Table Scraps

Poems from Society's Lunch Line

Serafina Rossi

BookLeaf
Publishing

India | USA | UK

Made with ❤ on the BookLeaf Publishing Platform
www.bookleafpub.in
www.bookleafpub.com

Dedication

These poems are wholly dedicated to you, Kiernan and
June, with all the love from my bandaged heart.

For all my kindred spirits
patiently waiting in the lunch line,
waiting for permission to be seen:
The invisible children of the family,
the invisible mothers of society,
the invisible (but ever criticized) millennials,
the invisible misfits
forced into a box,
pushed into a corner,
a lifetime of waiting in line for validation -
There's such beauty in stepping out,
and finding your own way 'round to the front.
I hope you find a little piece of it here
and carry it with you after the turn of the final page.

Preface

Serafina Rossi's collection of poetry in *Table Scraps: Poems from Society's Lunch Line* allows the ability to play with the boundaries of poetry's nonfiction loopholes and structural flexibility. *Table Scraps* combines the under-appreciated art of oversharing in group therapy with a sprinkle of dark wit and some uncomfortable honesty in a way that only the invisible child in a family can. Through this honest collection, the uncomfortable-but-all-too-common experiences of invisible individuals can allow them the validation and freedom to finally shove their way to the front of the societal lunch line with their stories: No longer content with politely waiting their turn in the back.

Serafina is the curious misfit: The kid in class who was always reminded to "get that head out of the clouds," the dramatic storyteller, high school English teacher, copywriter, and artist exhuming truth behind a collection of words - the raw honesty of art. Her artistic and written works are inspired by her own experiences, the experiences of others, and the journey towards finding the courage and the voice to confront them. *Table Scraps: Poems from Society's Lunch Line* explores the concept of truth through the eyes of the discarded, whispered tales of light and darkness, and the dichotomy of good and evil within us all.

Acknowledgements

This collection would have never been possible without the courage, resilience, and overflowing emotion that my children stirred within me from the moment they entered the world.

To my husband Chris, one of the lucky ones born at the front of the lunch line but always giving your place to others who weren't born as lucky: Thank you for being the exception to most of my poetry, and for proving to me that love doesn't have to be laced with toxic chemicals.

Writing has been my frenemy for years, but there have been some who never accepted my self-sabotage as reality. This collection is a nod to them and their beautiful souls. Specifically Anj and Danielle, who I can always count on for truth with compassion: My chosen sisters, who never ceased to see me and my potential these last thirty years beneath so many layers of self-doubt.

And for Eileen, who never allows anyone to go unseen and unheard.
Thank you for seeing.

1. Meetings

Voices blurred to white noise
Absorbed by clouds
Wrapped around my brain-
Scattered showers of words,
A handful of droplets
Soak the soil of memory
Piercing through the mist-
Trapped in obligation,
A statue caged by silent propriety.
Every nerve aches for activity
To shatter the marble-
Legs twitching,
Eyes frosted with crystallized boredom.
So I stay frozen in ice trays
Of social rules,
Doodling in a meeting-
The colors of freedom
Crafting life in the striped margins
Of a lifeless notebook.

2. Champagne and Donuts

The first time I disappointed you,
there were donuts and champagne,
a pink hospital basin
and a swerving wheelchair
steered by your eldest daughter.

I was birthed in sadness,
conceived in grief
over your father's life,
taken from you too soon.

I grew inside your sobs,
nourished in darkness-
taking root in a cold tomb of spring
and evicted in February ice.

Were you praying
to ancient gods you don't believe in
for the reincarnation of your father
through the tomb
you sculpted within?

Were you hoping
for a son,

the oil-on-canvas
still-life portrait of
your very Italian father -
the only person you ever truly liked?
                    -or
loved?

The first time I disappointed you,
an eager audience waited
to clink champagne flutes after my arrival,
toasting to a prayer answered,
a boy - after two daughters -
finally a son,
the visage of his grandfather,
painted with watercolor teardrops
on a blank canvas.

I emerged in a noose,
lips frigid purple and frostbite blue,
a room of chilled champagne flutes
overflowing with frozen
sighs.

The champagne lost its glitter,
the donuts hardened in stale hospital
air-

disinfectant and disappointment.

-and you,
 a shriveled seed sipping warm champagne,
 curdled bubbles of bile
 stagnant now on your tongue -
 nibbling glazed crumbs
 abandoned by frigid glances and
 stiff shoulders of the once eager audience.

Crumbling mother of three girls.
now
slumped in a swerving
wheelchair,
steered around hospital corridors
by your eldest of three.
three daughters.
now.

Still swerving,
you purge the flat champagne
the stale donuts
stale desires and
dreams dissolved in stomach acid -
Forced out of your body
into a pink hospital basin.

This last withered seed of hope-
  - of warmth -
  - of your love for this third daughter
now curdling in bile,
left behind inside a pink basin of
hospital waste.

3. Running Thoughts

Running alone in the darkness
Trees whispering secrets in the breeze,
Crickets respond,
Desperately wanting to be part of it.
Street-lamps flicker
Headlight eyes glance
In my direction and
Just as swiftly avert their gaze.
They don't see me
Making my way
Through shadow.
Shadow moving through shadow,
Whispering secrets to the trees
And averting gazes
Of eyes that glance my way,
Fleeting movements of shadow

in the dark.

4. Half Full

Optimism
creeps in corners
of red-rimmed eyes,
behind those dusty nooks
inside the mind.

Optimism lurks
inside cobwebbed attics,
musty basements.
Hope is usually stored there,
stuffed hastily inside boxes
labeled with faded marker
behind the peeling paint
of old Santa figurines,
hidden from view
by mold-coated board games
from my childhood,
and faded photographs,
faded relics of happiness,
faded relics
of a faded identity.

Raspy breaths scatter
tumbleweeds of dust,

fingertips sweeping cobwebs
from dampened cardboard flaps,
prying the frayed corners open
one last time.

I peek inside,
but quickly squeeze my eyelids shut,
terrified to find
the box contains
nothing.
I snap the cardboard flaps down,
head turned away.
They bend beneath the strength
of my hands,
they hardly put up a fight,
flaking and dissolving into pieces
beneath their firm grip.

I cast it skidding across the floor
with a shove,
send that creature back in the corner,
reuniting with cobwebs,
generations of dust
buried once more beneath
tangled knots of Christmas lights-
dolls with cracked faces,
old home videos on VHS tapes,

relics from a
deceased medium.

Old memories from
deceased dreams.

5. With Respect to Edgar Allan Poe

Re: The Pit and the Pendulum

Regarding your short story
of psychological, historical horror
(one of your most famous),
the narrator found himself
horrifically trapped within
the tragic depths of a pit
and tortured,
strapped to a plank,
drowning in darkness
inside an eternal pit of horror.
He claims,
"No! - even in the grave, all is not lost."

With respect to the narrator
and Mr. Poe,
who will remain my dark spirit twin,
my soul's angst eternally reflected
in his melancholy prose,
with respect, sir,
but I fear to inform you
that this narrator was

tragically mistaken.

For some narrators,
even in the grave
or out of the grave,
all is lost
before
their stories
even begin.

The pit is real,
the swinging pendulum above
will not conveniently caress
the restraints of a woman,
no friendly rats will chew her free,
inside a pit of promised freedoms.
Even freedom falls into nothingness
for some narrators.

When her own skin
entraps
ensnares
staring her down with
eyes that cast judgments
and eyes that lie
blaming her for the agony

of her body's own
shattered pieces.

Dangling her children
like carrots,
signing their birth certificates
with a mother's blood and
swinging the righteous pendulum
of men's rights
fathers' rights
politicians' rights,
cackling at other lost narrators
once strapped to planks before.

The political pendulum creeps closer.
"Give up your rights
and keep your life,"
they hiss in her ear.
She hopes for the freedom of sleep
the darkness of the ignorant,
the bliss of night
the bliss of easy choices
and falling into that
Pit,
falling into the nothing
below

for even falling is
preferable
for some of us
sometimes.

With all due respect, Mr. Poe,
even in death,
you're still a man
staring into a pit of your own
swinging a pendulum of your
own
with others like you,
others just like you,
in fact,
pointing sinister flames and
screaming accusations of
frail hysterics
from a frail woman.

Prying bodies open,
forcing things in
ripping things out
this is the true prison,
the pit we've lived in
from the moment

we're forced from the womb.

Who will emancipate these narrators
at the end of the story?

You now sleep blissfully
within the night of nothingness
from your drunken grave
but you never observed
the walls of women around you
closing in around them,
while scribbling your tales
of tragic men.

For some narrators above
this exhumed pit of womanhood,
buried alive within the fertile soil
the dirt of archaic prejudice,
in this man-made pit of horror,
our female narrators
are still lost at the end
of society's stories.

6. Beauty and Abuse

Ghosts of abuse victims
pass through beautiful
painted women
staring without sight,
unseen
unheard.

Mascara masks all
teary-eyed empathy,
hot pink smiles
conceal fangs
harsh side-eyes
sliding beneath
false lashes.

Questioning gazes
and whispered lies
slithering from
needle-plump lips
of abusers
and their cohorts
burrowing craters of doubt
with lasers to furrowed brows.

Painted pointing fingers
buttery-soft hands
clasped over dry mouths of honesty
and dry minds of deceit.

Blindfolded
bedazzled
ladies of justice
tipping the scales
with blood diamonds
mined with the betrayal
of other women.

Little painted puppets,
who's pulling your strings
and smearing rouge
to create those fake smiles?

7. Truth is a Powdered Wig

Truth is a powdered wig
sprinkling dust onto
cloaked shoulders of justice,
with a puff of confetti-shredded law
dripping glue from papier-mâché gavels.

These upholders of law,
shoulders shrugging
and upturned palms
stained with thirty silver pieces,
kissing victims on the cheek
and leaving lipstick stains
that can't be scrubbed clean,
Worshiping gold-plated
snake-charmers.

Idealized idols of justice
floating in diamond deprivation chambers
beneath charming masks of "good intentions"
while ripping voices from victims.

8. Hands

You always said,
"Never bite the hands that feed you."
Those hands -
-scraping, scooping, kneading, rolling
fingers that pinch rolls of dough
with disapproving glances -
- dough from thickening thighs, a plump behind
and babyfat cheeks
dough-ful with every critical hand-ful.

Those feeding hands waned thin each meal,
dinnerware shrinking and dough-less -
dwindling grains of worth
served with each heaping helping of puberty.

You always said,
"Idle hands are the devil's playthings."
Those hands -
- my father's hands, folded in idle prayer
- my mother's hand, raised in idle worship -
- the other hand yanking my idle childhood wrist
when I idly daydreamed on Sunday mornings
sitting idly stiff on a cold church bench.

On the other hand -
- someone's non-idle hands opened the trapdoor
of my personalized hell.
- there were some who kneaded these dough-ful curves
with rolling-pin hands flattening women on their backs -
- hands that pry knees open and
- hands that pinch mouths closed.

Didn't you always say,
"The truth will set you free"?
Now you sit idle there
with idle stares
and skeptical hands folded
under a cold kitchen table, asking
- what I did
- what I wore
- what I said
- what I didn't say.

I thought I was supposed to be *"set free"?*
Instead, darkness tightened its grip in my throat,
my mind a prison
my voice shackled to silence.

"Idle hands are the devil's playthings."
I've seen the hands of evil.
I've felt the devil's fingers around my neck,

and your idioms are empty-handed -
"*Bird in hand,*"
"*Hand over fist.*"
When I see hands that caress the heart
with gentleness,
loosening those frayed
gnarled knots of my past,
I sometimes think those hands are his.
Those hands become his hands
and his hands
and his hands too.

My hand was dealt -
my cards were on the table,
but you were always the dealer
and the idle house always wins.
You called a bluff that didn't exist
folded before the game was called -
pitter patter raindrop cards
scattered on the kitchen
table
from hands swollen with the dew of denial -

"*Too rich for my blood.*"
Peel the poker-face -
see the free-hand scarring the page
with these cutting words,

these carvings of my past
still blood-fresh on my skin
buried beneath the dust of passing years.

Up the ante, because I'm all in -
I've studied your bet for decades,
played by your idle house rules.

Now I'm biting the bluffing hands
that force-fed me those idle lies,
and I'm sorry it hurts -
- but that blood is on
   your hands.

9. Paradox 1

Force-fed motherhood
with spoons of self-sacrifice
and a prix fix menu of pain -
fatherhood remains a-la-carte.

Mothers spending lifetimes
proving their struggle is worth
table scraps society deigns to allow -
but can never enjoy,
too busy defending accusations
from a-la-carte foodie fathers.

Snapping at the help, these
sampling, savoring fathers
demanding course after course,
goblets of wine and servitude,
sitting high above mothers and children
from this societal Versailles
slurping *au jus* from gold platters,
forcing women to beg for bites
of a meal she never ordered
nor even had the peace
to pause and savor.

She's stuck with the bill
regardless.

10. Siren Song for an Airhead

Another Halloween comes to a close,
my children greet me with chocolate smiles
and pillow cases of saccharine loot
they generously offer to share.

I eagerly pillage the haul
for buried treasure,
and the brilliant silvery glow of those
nostalgic Airheads pique my interest —
— a siren call to my pirate mind
— especially the ruby reds,
 and those faded emerald greens,
 raspberry blue sapphires most commonly favored
 despite the confusion in name

Sparkling, sugar-prismatic flavors
including one other,
whose unknown secrets
beg to be discovered by the giddy *teenager- me*
— though she's foolish, she remains
ever the curious, inquisitive one:
White Mystery.

It appeals to me, that whispered promise:
Mystery.
14-year old me was drawn to the whisper, too,
just as she was drawn to the whispered promises
of the very first boy ever to pause,
to glance,
to see.
Cloaked in tantalizing question marks
eager to peel layers
a forbidden, almost dangerous adventure
in the mind of foolish *teenager-me,*
and so, he truly was a
white mystery
of whispered promises
and secrets fluttering
among airy stars.

Breathy promises of romance
dripping in candlelight,
and love letters scrawled in haste
under the scrutiny of our tired teachers —
every breathless moment silvery new
all so alluring
all so mysterious.
Expecting layers
sensitive and deep,
A sparkling question mark

concealing brilliance
under a smug facade.

Stripped of the foil wrapper,
a shiny mask of question marks
and alluring promises of depth
revealed nothing other
than skim-milk white.

Bland and blonde.
Simply artificially-flavored,
a vanilla strip of flat nothing —
void of color,
void of taste,
void.
This flavor that connects with nothing
and with no one.
This flavor that exists as nothing more
than brittle grains of sickeningly sweet sand
lingering on the tongue like battery acid,
eroding the calcium from bones and teeth
while bitter grains of slowly dissolving disappointment
erode the calcium from fortified happiness,

 A white mystery he was,
for the mere illusion of depth

behind the smoke and mirrors
of a bedazzled question mark
confused a ruse from truth
for this once intelligent teenager.

This silvery question mark draws me in
with whispered promises still,
though the wrinkled wisdom of experience —
and far too many broken hearts
has made me wary of secrets.
Even this version of me wonders of secrets
hiding beneath those siren-song question marks
still so mysterious on the foil wrapper.

Will it be different this time around?
Has the mystery finally changed?

Somehow, the wary version of me
succumbs to teenage-me curiosity
at the close of Halloween each year,
while I eagerly pillage the pillow cases
of loot from the trick-or-treat haul.
I sink my teeth into the first nostalgic bite.

Just another white disappointment —
the same white disappointment
year

after
year.

Wary me and *teenager me*
aren't really so different
after all.

11. Paradox 2

Why do I stare down
in disgust
at my own fleshy abdomen —
carved with a faint white scar
over skin stretched
like taffy?

Permanent badges of glory
branded on the body —
these ugly flaws
belong on display,
like trophies.

Trophies of strength,
resilience and
gritted teeth,
deep breaths
through flames of pain
no man could endure
quite so beautifully —

why do they pretend
to know the burn,
to feel the flames

to see for a lifetime
the searing-white scars
of self-sacrifice?

12. Social Media

It's not exactly impossible
or even that difficult
to find evidence that technology
dehumanizes humans,
strips us naked of human,
flesh and blood
brain and behavior
memories and feelings —
sadness,
adrenaline,
pleasure —
replacing human with
handheld insecurities.

Dollar signs showcasing our worth
flashing neon to the world,
glowing reminders of what we lack.

These portable political arguments,
the electronic ping-pong
back and forth
        and
           back
        and

forth
Handheld ego boosters
of portable knowledge
portable wit
and likes upon likes
for the stories told
in your photos,
portable dopamine.

Using these ego boosters
to *educate you,*
to validate you,
to rubber stamp your worth
in the world
by how much you post —
or how little you post —
"not very active on social media"
is a kiss of death
for anyone trying to get a job
or a date,
because those who are
"not very active on social media"
are only those who don't exist.
a social media basement haunted
by social ghosts.

Magnetized to devices,

these ego boosters,
checking replies to that
political post
texting friends about
the trolls in your comments
pushing buttons.

Or snapping photos of meals
cooked for your family with love —
— *but don't touch it until I take a photo*
and post it to my story! —
A warm meal for your family's dinner
now congealed and soggy
cold and inedible,
glued to a screen
boasting your culinary mastery
to the world.
Do you cook for your family
or for the likes?

Tweeting intriguing commentary
watching a show, a film,
or listening to a song
as you sit in silence
with muted commentary in your mind —
starving for conversation,
starving for touch,

starving for playfulness
and the caress of a person's lips.
Starving to live —
Starving to human.

Just when technology connects us
human to human
now more than ever,
loneliness lingers — so heavy, so thick —
like gloomy days in January
when we can't remember
or see any trace of
our last glimpse of sun.

Couches become bridges
stitched with wet blades of
brown, dying grass,
weaving humanity together
one non-human to another —
the weak spots grow wider,
facades begin to peel,
the glue loosens from our devices
shifting weight as we reach for our screens
to record this moment in our timeline —
before the heavy fog of loneliness
causes the collapse.

13. Questions, Unanswered

Society's questions for women:

Why don't you smile more?
Why are you always smiling?

Why is your hair so long?
Why is your hair that short?

Why don't you ever wear makeup?
Why do you wear so much makeup?

Why are you single?
Why did you marry him?

Why don't you want children?
Why did you have children with him?

Why are you so stubborn?
Why didn't you fight harder?

Why are you giving up on the relationship so soon?
Why did you ignore the red flags for so long?

Why don't you wear something more "flattering"?

Why did you wear "that" if you didn't want the
attention?

Why did you leave?
Why did you stay?

Why are you giving up without a fight?
Why did you put up with it for so long?

Why are you so emotional?
Why are you so cold?

Why don't you drink?
Why were you drinking?

Why are you so paranoid?
Why did you believe his lies?

Why do we fail even when we win?
Why do we fight the wave-pool of society?

Was the tide designed by men?
                    Or by us?

14. Paradox 3

Please.

I'm begging you.
I'm begging you to listen.
I'm begging you for empathy.
I'm begging you to stop
pretending to understand
the physical
the mental
the emotional
trauma and pain
of motherhood.

I'm begging you
keep your religion
keep your laws
keep your judgments
off my body.

Keep your standards
off my abdomen
and away from my thighs.
I've painted miracles
between them

but you only painted
a bloodstained palette of
invalidation
invisibility
insignificance.

I'm begging you to stop.
I'm begging you to change.
I'm begging you
for my daughter's sake,

Please.

15. Paradox 4

Who knew
bodies,
identities
could be traded
among men
like baseball cards?
stats on the back,
height, weight, cup size —
even "home-run" averages
increasing in value
the longer it's preserved
— but decreasing in value
if preserved on a dusty shelf
for far too long,
always pushed towards the back
to make room for newer,
less dusty acquisitions,
stagnant —
trapped in plastic sleeves
of man's leather-bound
prized collection.
awaiting freedom
from the box,
from being on display,

from being trapped in an album.

Who knew
we could be traded,
again
again
and again,
awaiting worth
inside plastic,
traded for generations
to the next buyer?

16. Paradox 4.1

Who knew
my own body
my own womb
the body's cyclic
protests of pain
would be a bag
over the head
ropes around my neck,
smothering and
strangling life
in hidden corners
that no one else
can see?

Who knew
pushing through
month after month
with painted smiles
feigned color on cheeks
and strategic black,
frequent restroom breaks
scrubbing scarlet from pants,
judgmental employers
raising eyebrows and

accusations of time theft
would be one more thing
you have to apologize for?

Who knew
women feel pressured
to apologize
while each month
forced to pretend
pain isn't real
that these smiles
aren't actually
concealing a pain
that society won't see,
a slow internal death
gasping for air?

17. Paradox 5

Society forces
reproductive rules
onto those
enduring all
reproductive pain

Yet
these rules
aren't forced
onto those
least affected
least inflicted
least impacted

Those deemed
most lucky
most fortunate
freedom through
entire lifetimes.

18. Paradox 5.1

Mothers will
spend her lifetime
defending herself
over-explaining herself
over-silent
overexposed
to accusations and lies
about herself,
repeating answers
to repeating questions
of whether she truly
deserves motherhood
while simultaneously
existing
without
a choice.

19. Letters to Anyone Listening at the Family Court

Dear Sir or Madam,

Protectors of children at your best,
Enablers of abuse at worst.
Knowledge of pen-and-ink laws
are generally useless here.
Pause.
Focus.
Family law has to be less robotic
saving children in custody battles
at best.
victim-blaming gatekeepers
at worst.
Focus, now.
Lift your eyes from the book
you might be pointing the finger
at another victim of abuse,
the parent speaking out
against an abuser
to protect their children.

Dear Sir or Madam,

Don't punish the voice of abuse,
don't lock the wrong parent
outside steel gates
inscribed with
Children's Best Interest
padlocks forged
in fires of trauma
jaded by the wolves
wearing red cloaks.
I admit,
the angel wings of family court
appear a bit tattered
shredded feathers littering cages
and demanding rent
to occupy spaces
of decay and
rotting loving homes
while fortifying
steel bars of the cage
abusers carefully built
for me.
for them.

Dear Sir or Madam,

so many parents
speaking out against abusers
now writhing in heartbreak
choking on the stench of gaslighting,
abusers bearing fangs
that pierce hearts of accusers
making the accusers accused
and the abusers abused
while decision-makers tie their hands
and take their leisurely time
forcing children and parents
to maintain a *status quo*
while you sip mai tais poolside
at the Florida Keys
families are stuck in misery
sinking in swamps of legal debt
suffocating on the *status quo.*
family court is a slow quicksand,
no one emerges alive
without wings.

Dear Sir or Madam,

I see fathers and mothers
fighting the past
bored and tired civil servants
perched on podiums of

powder-wig courts
pushing children
into the arms of abusers
believing they can change
believing parental rights
outweigh the risk -
the risk of harming children.

I see your pain.
It is my own.
I see your tears.
They are my own.
I see your hopelessness.
It is my own.
I see your resolution
To protect the *good dads*
(and very rarely
the *good moms*) -
Men like you.
Fathers like you.
This resolution is my own
to protect others like me.
Women like me.
Mothers like me.
Children like mine.
From bored and tired
civil servants

shrugging shoulders
taking a leisurely vacation
in the depths of a child's pain
and sipping mai tais
soaking in the warmth of sunshine
soaking up a well-deserved vacation
as victims of a forced *status quo*
pile on your podium.

Dear Sir or Madam,

I see you, Midas
turning pain to gold
coins dripping with blood
of those abused mothers
who you labeled as liars
and their abused children
who you labeled as unreliable.
I see you squinting at court ledgers
and balancing scales
of the abusers
versus the abused,
demanding taxes in
brackish tears and
pounds of flesh,
the price of freedom
chisels the portcullis

of these abusers.

You gift-wrapped the key
in trappings of your heartbreak
tossing it on the altar
of all wrongly accused men -
one more sacrificial lamb
for the ledger.

Focus, now.
You've lost focus, now.
You're a protector of children,
not an executioner
of abuse victims with voices.
Protectors don't balance scales
of good and evil -
yet you claim to protect
children's best interests
while convincing them
that they don't know reality,
while convincing them
they don't know love,
that reality isn't real,
that ice is warm
that fear is kindness
that masks are truth
that healthy love is a lie.

Dear Sir or Madam,

I mean no disrespect,
only to peel layers of truth
cloaked over rotting fruit of deceit
and twisted turns of phrase-
like sucking browned and bitter lemon rinds
long after the zest perished in its own ooze
breeding never-ending fruit flies.
Tongues coated in decay
stagnant acid dissolving teeth
until you're slurping nourishment
through a discarded straw
and robbed of your bite.

One Final Letter -
To the Abuser Spewing Lies in Family Court These Four
Long Years:

Dear Sir,

I have some bite left
to leave the faintest
crescent of a scar
on the alabaster ego
of abusers playing house

within the doors of family court
casting themselves as victims.
I'm not slinking away
at your drooling snarl
Now I snarl back.

My children are worth
all the acid-eroded bite
that remains in this
fiercely protective mother
who hasn't lost her voice.
I know this is uncomfortable
this truth is not often proper,
but I refuse to be another tool
used at the whims
of society's straw.
I slaughtered my body
for my children -
you contributed one
brief moment of pleasure.
My body fed them
bled for them
smelled my burning
flesh for them,
carved my heart and
elegantly arranged the slices
on a butcher's block for them,

and they know it.
They feel it.
You can keep snarling
but you know they know love.
They know love from me.
You know the children
that family courts are
required to protect
are smarter than you
wiser than you
better than you.

They know the truth
you refuse to confess:
That you, snarling, sniveling sir,
family court won't protect them
as you, sir, the rancid lemon,
ooze poison and vomiting lies
breeding all those fruit flies
in your wake.

Wipe the drool
from those watered-down victim tales
leaking from exposed holes in your story
Take off the dusty
red hood and cloak
of feigned innocence

and show the fangs
you only reveal in secret -
Remove your acidic bite
from my life once and for all,
and from my children's souls.

Regards,
The Woman Who No Longer Fears You

20. Teaching to the Test

Standardized testing
dissolving the fulfillment
of every educator's soul
a race purposely designed
by non-educators
and children-haters
to never have winners.

Chewing away the teacher's passion
with yellow teeth and sagging jowls,
spitting out the frayed remnants
and faded, underpaid memories
of the enthusiastic educator.

21. Family Portrait

In the blue room
with the blue walls
of memorialized degrees
and faded blue carpet,
those brown and grey stains
hidden cleverly under furniture,
and trash bins,
and potted plants
just after the eldest daughter
moved to New York
and the middle daughter left for college
(the blue room's prior tenants) -
You turned the blue room
into a blue study.

Industrial-aged electronics
unreliable and dusty
like the internet
birthed in my youth,
soon became the only home
that welcomed my voiceless words
instant messages from voiceless ghosts.

The framed family portrait hangs

tethered to the walls of the blue room
next to the memorialized college degrees
revered medical textbooks
and one swivel chair
so often finding myself
seated in and spinning around
waiting for the dusty computer
to connect to the dusty internet.

The family portrait stares into my eyes
with each spin of the swivel chair
Mother smiling
-spin-
Father smiling
-spin-
eldest daughter smiling
-spin-
middle daughter smiling
-spin-
their eyes meet mine
one
by
one
resentful
alienating
belittling
cold.

-spin-
Mother's eyes
dismissive and brown
like the wooden wall paneling
she always despised
in the living room,
her mother's decor
in her mother's house
and she, her caretaker
of her mother's house
the eldest of four
overlooked and resented.
She would have ripped the wood
paneling straight from the walls
with her small and steady
operating-room fingers until
her blood stained the wall's true color,
no trace of the past remaining,
only streaks of blood
bitter teardrops,
and old stains of resentment
hidden cleverly under new furniture,
new coats of paint,
trash bins
potted plants.
She stares at me now

in the blue room,
eyes dismissive and brown
wood paneling that resists
small,
steady,
operating-room fingers
clawing it free
from life's walls.
Resentment.

-spin-
Father's eyes
dark and haunted
like memories of abuse and ridicule,
his childhood alienation
fading behind generations
of masculine poison,
clouds of anger
concealing layers of hurt feelings
sadness and sensitivity
hidden cleverly under new furniture,
memorialized degrees
patents and accomplishments
trash bins
potted plants.
Boiled feelings turn sour
with emotional alienation

social alienation
a bullied child
stammering for strength
turned violent
an adult seeking validation
through wisdom and strength
turned religious.
Religious edicts dictate the terms,
an instruction manual
for social acceptance
through judgment of others.
Avoiding alienation
through alienation.
He stares at me now
in the blue room,
eyes dark and haunted
sour feelings
stammering for strength,
validation,
peace
clouded with trauma,
repressed anger
and masculine poison
Alienating.

-spin-
eldest daughter

the eyes of my sister
green and disarming
masking in bright charms
a lifetime of disappointment
the warmth of a summer day
in the middle of June
whispering promises
and secrets kept secure
in the breeze,
those eyes belittle you,
those labels of
"The pretty one"
and
"The super-model one"
and
"the only one to inherit
Your grandfather's light eyes"
they reduce you to nothing more
than eyes
and smiles
and promises
in the summer breeze.
How does a person change
the tides at the whim of
a moon?
How do the others that come
after you create their own tides

at the whim of
a mercurial family
whose own love fluctuates
with tangible objects
and appearances
that gradually wane?
My appearance was a crescent
from birth
my eyes
my smiles
hold no sway,
The brown hidden cleverly
beneath vibrant green potted plants
trash bins
even as appearances wane
with the tide.
She was the first,
the best of both
staring at me now
in the blue room
eyes green and disarming
secrets whispered in summer breeze
the best of both,
the glue for their marriage,
that unattainable pedestal,
Belittling.

-spin-
middle daughter
the eyes of my sister
eyes of cold granite
like the countertops so carefully
selected to complement
the fine Nordic cherry cabinets
in your fine
classic American
colonial home.
Granite so dense
even the sharpest blade
would not leave a mark-
smooth, flawless stone
the most expensive granite
in the most luxurious home
in the most luxurious neighborhood
cold.
Impenetrable perfection
reveals no wound
stains
neither fire nor ice
can weaken the surface,
neither love nor hate
can weaken that surface.
I often rest my cheek
on the cool stone

for relief,
flushed and damp
with the rising heat
of another family dinner,
red wine and
mindless dinner table chat
of who's who
and what's what,
complimenting compliments
between mindless mouthfuls
and mindful sips
mind-flaying words of depth,
of passions and truth
stretching the void
into mindless ears,
smooth, flawless stone.
She stares at me now
in the blue room,
eyes of flawless granite,
obsidian,
two exquisite countertops
impenetrable by humanity's blade
Cold.

-spin-
Ghost in a swivel chair
staring at the portrait's void

into the eyes of voiceless strangers,
spinning in a blue cave
a stain tucked away with
potted plants
trash bins,
a ghost in a swivel chair
staring at the family
that should have remained
as four.
This ghost
now seeks connections
with voiceless strangers.
The family portrait
of hollow dreams
genuine smiles
in the blue room,
the blue family
of broken smiles
and painted joy.

* 9 7 8 9 3 6 9 5 4 0 8 8 4 *